E3 Leadership

Why E + E + E = E

Written By
John Barrett

Published by
Rocket Publishing

Published By: Rocket Publishing

Book Design By: John Barrett Art

www.johnbarrettart.com

Thanks:

My amazing wife, Erin, our two beautiful girls, Zion & Allie, and our little man, Isaiah. They teach me more about leadership than anyone else ever could. To everyone who helped bring this book together with their appreciated input. To my mentor Dr. John C. Maxwell for showing me the way.

CONTENT:

E3————————————————————— 9

E1 - Engage Your Challenges——————————15
    E1.1 Admit You Have A Problem————————21
    E1.2 Back Away From The Problem——————25
    E1.3 Commit To The Problem————————31

E2 - Extract Your Solutions————————————37
    E2.1 Get Around The Right People——————39
    E2.2 Get Your Head In The Clouds——————45
    E2.3 Get Experimenting With Ideas——————51

E3 - Empower Your Performance————————59
    E3.1 Discover Yourself————————————63
    E3.2 Develop Yourself ——————————— 69
    E3.3 Discipline Yourself————————————75

Elevate Your Success——————————————83

Conclusion————————————————————89

E + E + E = E

E3 Leadership is a formula that will set you up for greater success if you follow the sequence. It is a progression that, when followed, will bring you to your desired outcome.

Everyone needs a plan for how they are going to maximize their possibilities, and E3 Leadership will give you that plan. It will lead you through the journey of how to identify your limiting challenges, creatively find solutions, and become a powerful leader that generates high levels of success.

Every leader also needs a guide to help bring out the best in them. Luke had Yoda, Katniss had Haymitch, Frodo had Gandolph, Dorothy had Glenda, Neo had Morpheus, and the list goes on. Everyone needs a trusted coach to help them become the hero they were created to be. I do just that. My role is to help you level up your leadership ability and win. Through speaking, writing, coaching, and training I guide leaders to the next level. When leaders go to a whole new level, their success goes to a whole new level. This book is designed to coach you through a process to help you reach your next level.

When asked about his country's greatest weapon against the Nazi regime, Winston Churchill didn't hesitate to reply, "It was what England's greatest weapon had always been…hope." What Churchill knew, and what all great leaders know, is that a leader's most empowering "weapon" is hope. It is unquestionably the strongest motivational force you can use. When hope fills the heart, dreams of a better future overflow into reality. Hope makes the seemingly impossible become possible. We begin to see opportunities that otherwise would have remained hidden. Capitalism itself is built on the premise of hope; the hope that your effort will bring you success. This book will give you hope and specific strategies to be, do, and have more. There is always a way to reach your potential no matter what challenges you are facing. There are no hopeless situations, just people who have lost hope. They just need the right guide to help them get to where they know they can be.

Allow me the honor to coach you through my E3 process that will enable you to engage your challenges, extract your solutions, empower your performance, and bring you elevated success.

$$E + E + E = E$$

Engage Your Challenges + Extract Your Solutions + Empower Your Performance = Elevated Success

Enjoy!

Engage Your Challenges

+

Extract Your Solutions

+

Empower Your Performance

=

Elevated Success

Engage
Your
Challenges

Engage Your Challenges

Author and businessman Max De Pree said, "The first step of a leader is to define reality." You can't move forward if you don't know what is holding you back. Most challenges that individuals and organizations are facing stem from lack of awareness of what is actually happening.

The only reason you or your company isn't moving forward is that there is a problem somewhere somehow. If there weren't a limiting factor, you would always be advancing. Remember Newton's law of motion: An object at rest stays at rest, and an object in motion stays in motion with the same speed and in the same direction unless acted upon by an unbalanced force. Challenges, big or small, cause an imbalance in forward motion. And the longer the problem exists, the slower you progress.

The first variable in elevating your success is about engaging your challenges. It's about identifying what is holding you down from moving up. Defining precisely what problems exist enable you to know just how to fix them. Most people know they have challenges, but they haven't clearly defined why they are. In order to fix a problem, you have to first know

> "In order to fix a problem, you have to first know why you have it in the first place."

why you have it in the first place. It isn't enough to know what challenges are in front of you; you have to know where they came from. Anyone can tell you there is a problem, but not many can accurately tell you why there is a problem.

Dealing with a challenge is one thing, but dealing with the root cause of the challenge is another. Many organizations put bandaids on their problems, but in doing so, they fail to resolve the systemic issues that caused the pain point in the first place. We too easily settle for a quick fix rather than getting to the heart of the matter.

Taiichi Ohno, the Japanese industrial engineer responsible for the Toyota Production System that revolutionized the manufacturing industry created a groundbreaking process for problem-solving. It is used by the most innovative individuals and companies worldwide. He created a technique called The 5 Whys. This technique can be used to find the root problem in any situation. The general premise is that it takes at least 5 Whys until you get to the true reason a problem exists. Let me give you an easy example of this in a coaching conversation I recently had with a client.

Me: What challenges you are facing right now that you want to fix?
Client: Well, I am always late to work, and it puts me behind on my workload. I just need to be more disciplined to get up earlier I guess.
Me: Why are you typically late to work?
Client: I always seem to sleep through my alarm.
Me: Why do you always sleep through your alarm?

Client: I guess it's because I go to bed too late and never get enough sleep, so I don't hear it.

Me: Why do you go to bed too late?

Client: Not sure...wait, now that I think about it, I am always working into the evening trying to get stuff done for my work.

Me: Why do you stay up late working on tasks for your job at home?

Client: There is never enough time in the day to get it all done, so I have to take it home.

Me: Why is there not enough time at work to get all your tasks done?

Client: I get distracted a lot in the office and jump from task to task without completing them.

Me: What if you had a game plan for your day before you started it and knew exactly what you need to accomplish, so you didn't have to bring work home?

Client: That would be amazing, I guess I wouldn't be late to work as much...and would probably have more time to finish tasks during the work day too.

Me: Well, let's work together to get a plan...

The original problem this client stated was being late to work. When I first asked, "why," he said it was because he slept through his alarm. I could have stopped there and said, "Well then, you need to get a louder alarm and stop sleeping through it." But that wouldn't have solved the root problem.

The problem wasn't lack of sleep; the real problem was a lack of clarity with his schedule and workflow. I could have easily stopped short of the root issue and just worked with him to get to sleep earlier, but he still would have been overloaded with work and probably wouldn't sleep well knowing he had unfinished tasks hanging over his head every night. It took me asking five why's before we began to see the cause of his lateness.

Let me give you another simple illustration of the 5 Whys:

Problem: You were driving to work, and your car broke down.

1st Why?: The battery died.

2nd Why?: The alternator stopped functioning.

3rd Why?: The alternator belt broke.

4th Why?: The alternator belt was well beyond its useful service life and had not been replaced.

5th Why?: The vehicle was not maintained according to the recommended service schedule.

Solution: Fix the root cause of the problem by implementing a maintenance schedule for the vehicle in accordance with the recommended service schedule.

It's a waste of time to throw solutions at acute symptoms rather than the chronic issue. Great leaders always dig deeper than others. They keep engaging the problem until they have uncovered the issue. They keep asking questions until they truly engage the root. Albert Einstein once said, "If I had an hour to solve a problem and my life depended on the solution, I would spend the first 55 minutes determining the proper question to ask, for once I know the proper question, I could solve the problem in less than five minutes."

The first step in going to the next level is figuring out what is keeping you from getting there. Engaging your challenges causes you to clearly know what you are dealing with in order to overcome them.

You cannot advance to new heights if you are being weighed down in old thinking. To change your thinking, you have to change your perspective. One cannot improve upon something they are unaware of. Remember, if you haven't identified why challenges exist you will never be able to solve them correctly. Great leaders ask more questions than they answer. They are always willing to go behind the surface and get to the depths of problems. French anthropologist and ethnologist Claude Levi-Straus said, "The wise man doesn't give the right answer, he poses the right questions." Be a student that is willing to engage root problems so you can eventually solve the symptoms.

> "You cannot advance to new heights if you are being weighed down in old thinking."

Here are the A, B, C's that you need to know about problems if you are going to be a great student of engaging your challenges: Admit you have a problem, back away from the problem, and commit to the problem. Let's break these down.

(E1.1)

ADMIT YOU HAVE A PROBLEM

The only thing worse than having massive problems is not having any problems at all. Seeking to live problem-free is actually a limiting factor that can inhibit your potential. You see, the bigger the problems you have, the bigger the potential there is. It's like the young man who asked his mentor, "What's life's heaviest burden?" The mentor responded, "Having nothing to carry."

Author Dr. Malcom Maltz said, "We are built to conquer environment, solve problems, achieve goals, and we find no real satisfaction or happiness in life without obstacles to conquer and goals to achieve." Big problems are what great people face. Small problems are what average people face. No problems are what lazy people face. Problems are a catalyst for growth. Aristotle said, "Criticism is something we can avoid easily by saying nothing, doing nothing, and being nothing." Big thinking creates big problems. And it is much better to have big problems than never to have any at all.

So, instead of resenting your problems, start embracing them with courage. If you allow your issues to win...you'll lose. The goal is to overcome your challenges by rising above and moving beyond them. I like how philosopher Alfred A. Montapert said, "Expect problems and eat them for breakfast." Stop wishing you had it easier and start working to become better. Change your mindset to admit that it's ok to have problems, but it's not ok to not have problems. Always remember that successful people have problems, they just don't allow their problems to have them. The longer you deny you have challenges, the longer you'll delay progress towards solving them.

Here are three tips to deal with problems:

BE HUMBLE

Innovative solutions require humility. Humility helps you realize you don't know everything. You only grow by admitting you don't know. Learning begins when pride ends. Coach John Wooden said, "It's what you learn after you know it all that counts." People who think they know how everything works never open themselves up to learning new information. If you think you already know everything there is to know, about whatever it is you think you know, you will never fully know it.

> "You only grow by admitting you don't know."

The greatest enemy of creativity is pride. The moment you think you know it all is the moment you'll stop growing. When you stop seeking new ways to innovate, you stifle your ability to produce greater results. Unfortunately, many people have stopped growing because pride blocks them from learning. It's only when we admit that we don't know, that we can hope to know more. Vernon Howard said, "Always walk through life as if you have something new to learn and you will." Humility is the key that unlocks creativity.

BE HONEST

Don't sugarcoat your challenges. Don't hide from having problems. When we try to cover up what is holding us back, it only backfires on us and everyone around us. Being honest about what is trapping you is the key to discovering the way out. You can't shrug problems under the rug and expect them to go away.

Honesty requires vulnerability and being vulnerable requires courage. In fact, the word courage comes from the French word Coeur, meaning heart. Courage comes from our heart. It takes heart to be an innovative person. In order to be a great leader, you have to display the courage to step out and be exposed. Honesty validates your character and builds your influence. True problem-solving thrives in honest and vulnerable environments.

BE HUNGRY

You become successful by creating an appetite for challenges. Growth organically generates challenges. And the more growth you experience, the more problems will arise. Don't get worn out with problems. Keep yourself healthy. Lean in and engage your problem-solving ability. Curiosity breeds courage.

I have met and coached many people who have stopped growing because they stopped being curious. You never lose if you never give up. Don't allow yourself to settle for average. When you settle for average, you surrender your potential for greatness. Keep your mind fertile to new ideas and new ways of thinking. Don't get so full of yourself that you stop moving forward.

REVIEW

E3 LEADERSHIP

E1 — ENGAGE YOUR CHALLENGES

(E1.1) Admit You Have A Problem

a) Be Humble
b) Be Honest
c) Be Hungry

BACK AWAY FROM THE PROBLEM

Have you ever wondered when the best time to deal with a problem is? How do you know when to tackle an issue? Timing is vital when it comes to making decisions and creating solutions.

Let me make it simple: the best time to deal with a problem is when you have dealt with yourself first.

Most people are too close to their problems to understand what they really are. The closer you are to your challenges, the less you can see past them. Challenges are neither big nor small in and of themselves. It's what you compare them to that makes the difference. For example: is your house big or small? Well, that's a relative question. Compared to a tiny house, it's big, but compared to a massive home, it's small. The challenges you are facing right now are only as big or small as to what you are comparing them to.

Unfortunately, most people view problems way out of proportion. It's like taking a quarter and holding it up one inch from your eye–it appears to be huge, blocking your view from everything. In reality, though, it's only less than an inch in diameter.

Never deal with a problem when you are still in the emotional debris caused by it. Never make decisions in the dumps. Will Rogers said, "When you find yourself in a hole, the first thing to do is stop digging."

You can't solve problems in the wrong state of mind. Deal with yourself before you deal with the problem. If you are angry, hurt, bitter, or frustrated at your problems, it can easily cloud your

> "Deal with yourself before you deal with the problem."

judgment. Don't react to problems...act on problems. Understand that the more emotionally invested you are into a challenge, the harder it becomes to solve it. You have to deal with your response to the problem before you can deal with the problem itself. You have to stay cool and be alert. Make sure you are preemptively keeping yourself physically, emotionally, spiritually, and socially healthy. The more you do to keep yourself sharp, the greater the margin you have before you lose yourself.

Follow my three R's formula for when problems occur.

RETREAT

The first thing we must do when problems occur is to step back and retreat. Make sure you are in the right mind before you engage challenges. Step back and slow down before you or someone else makes a knee-jerk reaction. You can't deal with challenges when you're caught up the middle of them.

By simply stepping back from the situation, you will be amazed at the clarity it can bring. Get away somewhere that you can collect your thoughts. Better to act thoughtfully than to act recklessly. Don't be afraid to take a break and remove yourself from the situation.

REFUEL

Before dealing with problems, you are going to need the energy to break through. Don't try to engage problems when you are at your lowest. Refuel your emotional tank so that you have enough gas to make it through the solving process. When our energy is low, our mind is limited. It's jarred out of focus.

Never face a challenge without being prepared for it as well as you can. For every challenge you meet, you should have an equal refueling opportunity. Pour into yourself first so you can pour out your best to others. Face problems on a full tank. This is why it is vital to start each day with something that will fill your tank.

RESUME

Only when you are focused should you reengage with your challenges. When you have properly energized yourself, you can then be ready to tackle a challenge. The healthier you are, the faster you can resume where you left off. It's incredible how our physiological wellbeing can affect our ability to problem solve.

Don't return prematurely if it is in your control. Jumping back into a problem without being prepared for it can cause things to unravel even faster. Resume when you have resolved your focus and energy. Approaching a problem correctly can mean the difference between creating more problems or creating better solutions. Resume when you're ready.

REVIEW

E3 LEADERSHIP

E1 — ENGAGE YOUR CHALLENGES

(E1.1) Admit You Have A Problem
a) Be Humble
b) Be Honest
c) Be Hungry

(E1.2) Back Away From The Problem
a) Retreat
b) Refuel
c) Resume

E1.3

COMMIT TO THE PROBLEM

You can't allow your problems to derail your progress. When you stop trying to break through, you'll eventually break down. Understand that you will be tempted to quit when you face obstacles.

Whatever road you are on you can rest assured that there will be problems. In fact, the road of success is paved with obstacles. Only the ones that keep on keepin' on truly make it to the end. The good news is that the more problems you navigate through, the easier it is to deal with them. You get stronger and stronger after each victory. This is why highly successful people keep incredibly calm when facing big problems while others freak out.

If you remain faithful to keep pressing on you will become better and wiser after each issue you tackle. Difficulties don't exist to make life harder; they exist to make us stronger. Consider it part of the initiation to success. Einstein said, "It's not that I'm so smart, it's just that I stay with problems longer." Don't bail out and surrender too quickly–be committed for the long haul.

Here is how we can commit to breaking through problems:

BE PATIENT

Commit to being a problem solver for life. The path of success is not one of smooth seas and a warm breeze. Patiently persist by working challenges out over time. Don't expect everything to change overnight. Remember, it's those who have the stamina to last that become the winners.

If you don't have an unwavering sense of determination, you will give up when things get shaky...and things always get shaky. Radio personality Paul Harvey used to say, "You can tell you're on the road to success; it's uphill all the way."

BE PERSISTENT

Sometimes it's the tenth time you've engaged a problem that you have the one moment of breakthrough. Persistence is a trait of the successful. The secret to overcoming is to outlast your challenges. You have to have a strong sense of commitment not to allow a problem to get the best of you. Never give up until you have engaged a challenge to its core. Keep digging in until you hit the root and don't let up until then.

> "The secret to overcoming is to outlast your challenges."

Michael Jordan said, "If you're trying to achieve, there will be roadblocks. I've had them; everybody has had them. But obstacles don't have to stop you. If you run into a wall, don't turn around and give up. Figure out how to climb it, go through it, or work around it."

BE PASSIONATE

You won't stay with a problem unless you are passionate to solve it. Half-heartedly approaching a challenge will never get you to the other side. You need to connect your effort to a strong sense of why the problem must be solved. The higher the stakes, the more likely you are to stay with it. The lower the stakes, the less likely you will be committed.

Connect the dots of why the problem must be solved, and you'll develop the grit to get through it. Clearly identify your "why" and it will fill your tank with passionate energy to the solution. Leonardo da Vinci said, "Where the spirit does not work with the hand, there is no art."

Once you've properly engaged your challenges and identified why they exist, you can move on to solving them.

REVIEW
E3 LEADERSHIP
E1 — ENGAGE YOUR CHALLENGES

(E1.1) Admit You Have A Problem
        a) Be Humble
        b) Be Honest
        c) Be Hungry

(E1.2) Back Away From The Problem
        a) Retreat
        b) Refuel
        c) Resume

(E1.3) Commit To The Problem
        a) Be Patient
        b) Be Persistent
        c) Be Passionate

(E2)

Extract
Your
Solutions

Extract Your Solutions

Charles Kettering said, "A problem well stated is half-solved."

Extracting your solutions is about creating a strategy to break through your limiting factors. When you have correctly identified why your challenges exist, the path to bring change becomes clearer and more apparent. And when it comes to solutions the more options, the better. You have to spend time working through what I call, "Possibility Pathways." Possibility Pathways are potential options that could solve your challenges. Breaking down your solutions into multiple possible pathways helps you objectively asses options as you explore the outcomes. There is more than one way to lead and navigate to the next level. This is why examining the possibility pathways helps you know the best course of action.

Many people never take the time to plan out every possible solution. As a result, they get stuck engaging their challenges and never extract the right strategy to rise above them. They are frantically trying hard to find the one path and in doing so fail to see all the other options.

You don't just find solutions; you create them. This means there is a craftsmanship to being a great decision maker. Break-

> "Breakthroughs don't just happen; they happen progressively."

throughs don't just happen; they happen progressively. It's through options that we can clearly measure the best road to a solution. Businessman J.P. Morgan said, "No problem can be solved until it is reduced to some simple form. The changing of a vague difficulty into a specific, concrete form is a very essential element in thinking."

Let me take you through the extracting process by creating possibility pathways to gain clarity on the best solutions to move you and your organization to the next level. Henry Ford said, "Most people spend more time and energy going around problems than in trying to solve them."

There are three ways to extract solutions: Get around the right people, get your head in the clouds, and get experimenting with possibilities. Let's break these down:

GET AROUND
THE RIGHT PEOPLE

If you surround yourself with small thinkers you will always find yourself surrounded with unsolvable problems. But when you surround yourself with big thinkers unsolvable problems become solvable. The problem didn't change, but your ability to think through them did.

If you want to breakthrough challenges you have to have an inner circle that can help you. Lyndon B. Johnson said, "There are no problems we cannot solve together, and very few that we can solve by ourselves."

If you are facing a problem who do you go to? Who are the people that you surround yourself with that help you extract solutions?

Everyone should have someone that they can go to. If you don't have someone you can go to…your mission is to find that someone and develop the relationship. We were built for community. Your creative success will be dependent upon the people you surround

> "Everyone should have someone that they can go to."

yourself with. If you don't have a creative team to help you, you will limit your possibilities.

Collaboration breeds creativity.

Creative people have a tendency to act alone. They do well while working solo but have a hard time playing with others. It's not that they don't like other people, it's just that they feel others slow them down. Creative people don't like having to explain themselves and convincing others about their ideas. They just want to do what they do without anything getting in their way.

There is nothing wrong with wanting to move fast and avoid obstacles, but when we cut people out of the problem-solving process we end up cutting our effectiveness down as well. Creative people can create great things by themselves, but imagine how much more they could create with others. The truth is, the more collaboration, the more creative we can be in the long run.

It's said that 2 Horses can pull about 9,000lbs. together. How much do you think 4 Horses can pull? You would assume 4 Horses are able to pull 18,000lbs. however, 4 Horses can pull over 30,000lbs. together. Teamwork doesn't double your effort, it multiplies your effort. There is a compound effect that occurs when creative collaboration takes place. If you truly want to multiply your impact you must work well with others. Going solo limits your potential. When you work alone you have to work 10x as hard to produce.

Don't be afraid to lean on others and invite them into problem-solving conversations. Never solve problems alone. Always bring your inner-circle close to the issues so you can rely on their input and perspective.

Make sure you are surrounded by the right people, who think big and think for solutions.

If you are going to commit to being a great problem-solver you need to make sure you surround yourself with the right people. Those you surround yourself with can make or break your future.

Having the wrong people in a brainstorming session can kill the potential before there is even a possibility of greatness. If ideas get around what I call "Innovation Assassins" potential ceases to exist. We have all been targeted by "Innovation Assassins" who shoot down every good idea there is.

This is why we need to share our ideas (at first) only with those who have the ability to foster them and not squelch them. You have to have the right people working on the right problems or you'll get the wrong solutions. David Strauss said, "If you can't agree on the problem, you won't agree on the solution."

> "You have to have the right people working on the right problems or you'll get the wrong solutions."

Let me share this formula when it comes to brainstorming with the right people…

WRONG IDEA + WRONG PERSON = DISASTER

If you have a wrong idea that is no good and you share it with the wrong person it may actually end up happening. And the result is an unsuccessful endeavor that was a waste of time. Make sure you share brainstorming time with the right kind of people who are the right fit for the solution. Seeking counsel from the wrong people gives you the wrong ideas. If the person is unqualified or uninterested in the process don't allow them to speak into the solution. Not everyone should be asked their opinion about specific matters.

RIGHT IDEA + WRONG PERSON = DEATH

Having a great idea that is shared with the wrong person can knock the wind out of your sails. Skeptical, non-dreaming, realist, unmotivated, no life, fearful, problem finding, negative, purposeless people will bring death to great ideas. These people fight against every idea always picking out the bad. They kill ideas before they even have a chance to live. They're the kind of people who have a problem for every solution. Stay clear of people who habitually kill ideas with always pointing out the problems.

WRONG IDEA + RIGHT PERSON = PRACTICALITY

Sharing a wrong idea with the right person is wonderful. They are able to speak truth and practicality into the situation. You may have ideas that are just not very good. Having the right person who can help decipher the quality of an idea is a great thing that will enable progress. They will entertain the idea, but also help you work through better ideas. They will seek to build on your ideas not just tear them down. They tend to help you think through your wrong idea by asking great questions that get you to the right idea.

RIGHT IDEA + RIGHT PERSON = POSSIBILITIES

This is where the magic happens…when you have the right idea with the right person. This is where synergy and collaboration collide. This is where dreams are nurtured and built upon. Success lives in this equation. Always seek the right people with a track record of the right ideas in order to move quickly. Chemistry is necessary for collaboration. Seek out those who you can work together with and spend time with them. Be proactive about meeting consistently with the right person so you can come up with the right ideas together.

REVIEW

E3 LEADERSHIP

E2 — EXTRACT YOUR SOLUTIONS

(E2.1) Get Around The Right People

a) Wrong Idea + Wrong Person = Disaster
b) Right Idea + Wrong Person = Death
c) Wrong Idea + Right Person = Practicality
d) Right Idea + Right Person = Possibilities

GET YOUR HEAD
IN THE CLOUDS

Albert Einstein said, "We cannot solve our problems with the same thinking we used when we created them." To solve our problems we have to rise above them with a fresh mindset.

We have all heard the realists say, "Get your head out of the clouds!" But great leaders live the opposite–they get their head in the clouds. Great ideas come from seeing the big picture. And when you get your head in the clouds, you are rising up to high-level thinking. Breakthrough ideas come from thinking bigger than what everyone else thinks and beyond what everyone else is willing to believe.

In order to extract solutions, you have to operate beyond your challenge, bigger than your challenge, and bolder than your challenge. You have to get your thinking at a whole new level. Don't get weighed down in limiting thinking that is buried in trying to figure out how everything will work. Every person who has ever had a brilliant idea never knew how it was going to happen at first. In fact, if they would have started with the how question, it would have killed the idea before it even had any lift-off. The worst question to ask when you or others are birthing ideas into being is "How?" If great ideas always came with how they probably wouldn't be that great to begin with. We have to replace the "How?" with "Wow!"

I have attended many brainstorming sessions that dried up because too many people were asking "How?" before they let the ideas get some "Wow!" The preemptive "How?" questions kill creativity. It literally massacres greatness in the womb of gestation. The idea gets aborted because "How?" is asked too quickly and too critically. Great ideas aren't great at first; they need time to be wowed. The best way to shut down innovation and creativity is to start asking "How?" before you start saying "Wow!"

> "The best way to shut down innovation and creativity is to start asking 'How?' before you start saying 'Wow!'"

Here are 3 things you need to know about howing and wowing ideas:

"WOW!" IDEAS TO LIFE

Albert Einstein said, "If at first, the idea is not absurd, then there is no hope for it." Innovation derives from absurdity. Dreaming beyond our capacity is the catalyst for creativity. The greater the ideas we have, the greater the impact we can make. One is limited not by their bank account, friendships, or even opportunities, they are limited by the size of their ideas. Great innovators are great dreamers. Those that have made the biggest impact were the ones who were bold enough to envision unbelievable things. Eleanor Roosevelt said, "Great minds discuss ideas; average minds discuss events; small minds discuss people."

The greatest buzz kill in creativity is critical judgment. In fact, the more critical you are, the fewer ideas you will generate. Critical judgment cast a can't-be-done verdict before an idea even has a chance to present itself. Critical thinking is good, critical judgment is bad. If you knew how you were going to do everything before you did it, you wouldn't do very much in life. When have you ever known how you were going to do everything before you started? Never! No one ever knows all the answers on the front end. You have to wow ideas by giving them time to develop and soar before you assassinate it with how. Fan the flame of creativity in you and the others around you.

ASK "HOW?" ONLY AFTER "WOW!"

Leadership is all about timing. In "The Gambler," a hit song in the 1970s, Kenny Rogers sang, "You've got to know when to hold 'em, know when to fold 'em. Know when to walk away, and know when to run." As it turns out, this is profound wisdom not just for gambling, but for leadership as well. You've got to know when it's acceptable timing before you start shooting holes in an idea. Asking the right question at the wrong time can kill innovation.

• The proper question done at the improper time causes reluctance to an idea.
• The improper question done at the proper time causes resistance to an idea.
• The proper question done at the proper time causes resonance to an idea.

Timing is critical if you want harmony and resonance with an idea. If you get the "How?" before the "WOW!" you eliminate possibilities and create dissonance. Be ready to keep doing the same things because you'll never break out of the status quo when "How?" is asked first. "How?" is a great question, but only when it is presented at the right time. Only when you have let the idea be heard can you know what to truly ask. Waiting for ideas to fully expose themselves may change the questions and concerns you initially have.

You have to know the "How?" eventually, but it must be asked in the right sequence. Mess up the sequence and you'll mess up the creative flow. Too many life-altering ideas are lying dead on a conference room table because they were shot down in mid-flight by Howers.

BE CAREFUL HOW YOU ASK "HOW?"

"How?" is a great question at the right time and if the tone is correct. Say, "How?" with a positive tone, and you'll get positive results. Say it with a negative and critical tone (cue the eye shrug), and it will be the death of possible greatness.

In fact, studies have shown us that the tone in which people feel they are being communicated with will determine their response. It's not just what we hear, but how we hear it said that impacts us. The University of Southern California conducted a two-year study on the effects of tone in communication. They put married couples through therapy sessions monitoring the pitch and intensity of their voices. The computer algorithm analyzed the data and, surprisingly, was a more accurate indicator of marital success than counseling professionals. After a five-year follow up with the participants, the computer algorithm was able to accurately confirm eventual improvements or declines in relationships 74% of the time.

How we use our words determines a great deal of the results we get. The tone in which you ask "How?" makes the difference between continual progress or continual problems. When you let criticism and cynicism guide your how questions, you'll destroy the dreamers in the room. If you are incapable of asking "How?" with optimism and possibility, don't bring it up. "How?" is a brilliant question when asked with a how-can-we-make-it-happen attitude rather than a that-is-stupid-and-frankly-I-would-like-to-punch-all-of-you-for-coming-up-with-the-idea attitude. Your tone will either breath life into the idea or kill it; the choice is yours.

REVIEW

E3 LEADERSHIP
E2 — EXTRACT YOUR SOLUTIONS

(E2.1) Get Around The Right People
   a) Wrong Idea + Wrong Person = Disaster
   b) Right Idea + Wrong Person = Death
   c) Wrong Idea + Right Person = Practicality
   d) Right Idea + Right Person = Possibilities

(E2.2) Get Your Head In The Clouds
   a) "Wow!" Ideas To Life
   b) Ask "How?" Only After "Wow!"
   c) Be Careful How You Ask "How?"

GET EXPERIMENTING WITH IDEAS

Some of the greatest discoveries of our time have come through experimenting with the unknown. It is in the exploration of new ideas that we uncover unknown possibilities. Just imagine if the early explorers would have stopped exploring, or inventors stopped inventing, or artist stopped creating. All greatness comes from the willingness to step out and experiment with new mediums.

If you want to go further, you will have to experiment, no matter what field of work you are in. This experimenting may come in the form of ideas, business opportunities, finances, relationships, etc... If you want to experience new possibilities, you have to be willing to try new approaches. Never get stuck in the mode of always doing what you've always done. Don't get stale with the medium you currently use. If you are going to extract solutions you have to be willing to break out of normalcy.

> "If you want to experience new possibilities, you have to be willing to try new approaches."

Here are some tips to help you experiment:

DON'T STOP PLAYING

Start to tinker around with new ideas, new systems, and new opportunities. Begin to think outside the box that you've historically thought in.

Take a specific topic, start to study it, and see what others are doing. Bunny trail down the road of absurd and outrageous possibilities. Don't limit your thinking just because it is beyond your current level of awareness. Most people kill innovation in their life by dismissing anything that is beyond what they think they can do.

True innovators push their limits. They aren't afraid to playfully experiment with what might work. In fact, most innovative breakthroughs were not calculated and detailed on the front end, they evolved and morphed into what we know it as today from something very different to start with.

For example, in his book *Creativity, Inc.* Ed Catmull, the President of Pixar and Walt Disney Animation Studios, wrote about how the hit movie Monsters, Inc. began as the story of a 30-year-old, unemployed accountant who sees monsters that no one else can see. They turn out to be the fears he never dealt with as a kid. But the film took a needed change of direction as they begin working through it. He also tells of how the main character, Woody, in the movie Toy Story was originally created as a total jerk. But screen testers were appalled as they watched his mean personality. They ended up changing him to be the lovable character that he is today–voiced over by Tom Hanks.

You can't get to level three without walking through levels one and two. Success is a journey that takes trial and error. If you aren't willing to play, you won't go very far.

DON'T FEAR FAILURE

If you fear failed experiments, you will never try new things. If you are afraid to lose, you will never truly win. Greatness requires some sacrifices.

Two specific sacrifices are fear and pride. All negative forces stem from those two elements. Fear will tell you that it will never work, and pride will reinforce that statement by saying you'll be viewed as a failure when it doesn't work. Fear and pride are siblings that taunt your potential. You'll never extract solutions if you allow these two bullies to determine your possibilities. They control most people, but successful people sacrifice them on the altar of productivity.

Failed experiments are how you journey to greatness. Understand that failure is not bad unless you make it bad. In and of itself failure is neutral, it's what you do with it that makes the difference. Failure can be the best thing that happens to you. You can see it as a roadblock or a stepping stone…your choice. If you see it as a roadblock, you will avoid it at all cost and eventually come to fear it. However, if you see it as a stepping stone, you'll be free to try new things and learn from it as you become better as a result of it.

Failure is not fatal; it is simply part of the growth process to success. Robert Kennedy said, "Only those who dare to fail greatly can ever achieve greatly." It's comfortable to play it safe, but playing it safe is actually the riskiest place to be. Never be afraid to experiment with your future for the sake of being comfortable with your present.

DON'T STOP TESTING

Experiments take trial after trial after trial because that's how we learn. A child would never learn to walk if they didn't keep falling again and again. It is through the experiences of falling that a child discovers how to maintain balance and develop the strength to walk. If you give up every single time something goes wrong, you will never open the door to new possibilities.

Most new opportunities don't manifest after the first door you walk through…it is through the first door that leads to another…that leads to another…that leads to another…that leads to great potential. If you stop too short, you will miss something amazing. You have to first get a result in order to improve the result.

If you are going to get to the great, you have to travel through the bad, the average, then the good. There is a great statement I heard years ago that says, "You can easily become an overnight success after 20 years of hard work."

Success is a journey lived out step by step, by step, by step. You don't always make giant leaps; you make steady progress day by day. Even though you may have tried many possibilities, don't stop trying more things. You never know how far away you are from the right solution. I often say, "You are only one idea away from a major breakthrough." Thomas Edison said, "When you have exhausted all possibilities, remember this – you haven't." Breakthroughs happen for those who don't breakdown when they hit a wall.

"You are only one idea away from a major breakthrough."

REVIEW

E3 LEADERSHIP
E2 — EXTRACT YOUR SOLUTIONS

(E2.1) Get Around The Right People
a) Wrong Idea + Wrong Person = Disaster
b) Right Idea + Wrong Person = Death
c) Wrong Idea + Right Person = Practicality
d) Right Idea + Right Person = Possibilities

(E2.2) Get Your Head In The Clouds
a) "Wow!" Ideas To Life
b) Ask "How?" Only After "Wow!"
c) Be Careful How You Ask "How?"

(E2.3) Get Experimenting With Ideas
a) Don't Stop Playing
b) Don't Stop Failing
c) Don't Stop Testing

(E3)

Empower
Your
Performance

(E3)

Empower Your Performance

Johann Wolfgang von Goethe said, "If you would create something, you must be something."

Empowerment is about improving your ability to lead yourself and others effectively. How you go through your leadership journey is just as important as what you go through. Being empowered to operate at your best enables you to experience the best.

The hardest person you will ever lead is yourself. Theodore Roosevelt once stated, "If you could kick the person in the pants responsible for most of your trouble, you wouldn't sit for a month." As a leader, you have to work on you before you can work on them. You cannot expect to challenge others if you are not challenging yourself. If you are having trouble motivating yourself, you will have an extremely hard time motivating others. You can't lead the masses if you can't lead yourself.

To be a great leader you have to conquer yourself first. You have to come to a place where you slay your fears, self-worthlessness, failures, pride, worries, and limits. The best leaders are the ones who are confident in who they are. Not because of ego, but because of healthy self-assurance. Philosopher Lao Tzu said, "He who conquers men is strong; he who conquers himself is mighty." When you exterminate the enemy within, you liberate the warrior inside.

> "When you exterminate the enemy within, you liberate the warrior inside."

Leading yourself is about eliminating self-damaging beliefs that limit your ability to influence others. You cannot expect confidence and courage in others if you are not confident and courageous yourself.

To win in life and leadership, you have to bring your best self to your biggest challenges. Bringing your best self requires you to ask the question, "What would a great leader do?" This compelling inquiry empowers you to remove your bias and act appropriately.

Leaders have to be what they want to see in others. The most effective form of leadership is to exemplify the expectations you have in others. The values of an organization are not read on the walls of a building, they are read in the behaviors of the leader. So goes the leader's actions so goes the team's performance. If you do not like what you see in your people, you may need to change the way you are leading yourself. Empowering your performance is about reaching into the potential within. When you are at your best, your organization will be at its best. There is greatness within you that is eagerly waiting to be unleashed to a new level.

You have the potential to be an incredible leader, but it has to start with yourself. You cannot hide from the responsibility of self-leadership. You cannot fake it till you make it when it comes to authenticity. Your true self will come out in due time; therefore, you have to deal with your inner-limits if you want to have significant influence. When you conquer yourself, you can overcome anything. Rise up and slay the unwanted traits within yourself and begin to form the right thinking and habits to lead from your fullest potential.

To lead from your fullest potential you're going to first need to discover yourself, then develop yourself, and finally, drive yourself.

Let's break these down:

DISCOVER YOURSELF

"Know Thyself" was written on the forecourt of the Temple of Apollo at Delphi according to Greek writings. This saying became known throughout Greek culture as it spread throughout western philosophy. It continues to impact people and give us a great starting point for self-awareness. And in the context of leadership, it is true that you have to know yourself in order to be effective.

If you don't know who you are how will you know how to be your best? You can't. It's only through the self-discovery process that you truly align with your potential. The more you know yourself, the more you can grow yourself.

You should become an expert on who you are. You should know yourself better than anyone else knows you. Philanthropist Bernard Baruch said, "Only as you do know yourself can your brain serve you as a sharp and efficient tool. Know your own failings, passions, and prejudices so you can separate them from what you see."

Here are three ways you can know yourself:

KNOW YOUR PERSONALITY

We are all hard-wired in a specific way in which we operate. A method in which we function. Your personality is a combination of the character and traits that make you a unique person.

The good news is that you get to choose the traits you'll live by. People do not just end up somewhere in life; they end up where their personality took them. The traits you choose to live by become like an inner compass directing your future. People are not just a product of their environment; they are a product of their thinking. Author James Allen said, "You are today where your thoughts have brought you; you will be tomorrow where your thoughts take you." The way you approach life will be filtered through who you are—your personality.

Personality is defined as the combination of characteristics or qualities that form an individual's distinctive character. It's the invisible attributes that make us who we are. And who we are ultimately determines what we do. You see, who we are on the inside will always regulate what we do on the outside. So goes our internal being, so goes our external doing. This is why we are called human beings and not human doings.

> "So goes our internal being, so goes our external doing."

German poet Johann Wolfgang Von Goethe said, "Before you can do something you must first be something." Our doing is an overflow of our being. Everything starts within us and then works its way out of us. Thoughts develop inside our mind and then begin to move towards action. This is why it is so essential to develop who we are so we can improve what we do.

The more you know your personality and leverage it, the more you can empower your performance.

KNOW YOUR POWERS

Like all superheroes possess superpowers, we too, all have superpowers. Our superpowers are our unique strengths. They are the skills we inherently possess. The more we can grow our strengths the more we can make a difference. But you can only improve that which you are aware of. So, if you are unaware of your strengths, how will you ever know how to improve them? How will you know what to aim for if you haven't clearly identified your target? Self-awareness allows you to expedite your influence. Remember, the more you know yourself, the more you can grow yourself.

Years ago, I dedicated a few months to identify the strengths I possessed. It was a process of self-discovery as I worked to narrow my focus. I had been increasingly spreading my duties thinner and thinner as I was involved in too many roles. I finally had to have a meeting with myself to define who I was and where I should be investing my effort. Instead of being a jack-of-all-trades-and-master-of-none, I wanted to be a jack-of-few-trades-and-a-master-of-some. Through self-reflection, I realized there were three areas where I added the most value:

- ◦ Communicating
- ◦ Coaching
- ◦ Creating

I call them my "3C Strength Zone." I realized that these three areas were the things I not only should be spending at least 80% of my time in, but they were also the areas I needed to grow in. Instead of improving my weaknesses from terrible to average, I decided to upgrade my strengths from good to great. Instead of winging it in my strength zone, I decided to focus my time and energy to exploit it intentionally. I now have a target I know to be aiming for in order to help me focus my time and value. As soon as I get out of the 3C Strength Zone, I know I am wasting precious time and not adding the true value I can. This clarity allows me to adjust and re-shift my effort. My schedule is now filled with the majority of my time being dedicated to my strength zone.

If I were to ask you what your strengths are, you should have an immediate answer. You should be able to quickly and confidently give me a detailed response of precisely what you do best. If you fumble around and need paragraphs of articulation, you don't know your strengths. If you can't explain what you do best in a few sentences, you haven't taken the time to know your strengths.

KNOW YOUR PURPOSE

The most significant treasure a person can possess is the gift of purpose. Purpose gives us meaning and leads us to action.

One of the most profound questions we all ask at some point in our life, if not many times, is, "What is my purpose?" We can sometimes feel overwhelmed by this big question. We can get bogged down in the stress of trying to find out what we are meant for. Sometimes it can feel like we are searching for a needle in a haystack.

We hear from motivators that we need to "find our purpose!" So, we hope that one day we will wake up and stumble upon our destiny. We ponder the deep, "What is my purpose" question over and over. But there has to be more than just hoping to find our purpose—more than just searching for some hidden meaning.

I believe we are asking the wrong question. I have found that there is a better question to ask than, "What is my purpose?" The better question to ask yourself is, "Am I living with purpose?" We don't discover our purpose we determine it.

No one discovers their purpose as though it is out there waiting for them somewhere. It is something that you create. You see, we are created with purpose. We are designed for meaning. It's not that some have it and some don't. Everyone has purpose hard-wired within them from the beginning. Successful people live from purpose, while the unsuccessful are waiting for it. Purpose doesn't come upon us; it comes from within us. You get to determine what your unique purpose is.

Spend some time clearly articulating what you feel your unique purpose is. For example, my simple purpose statement I have come up with for myself is:

To live out my potential by helping others live out theirs.

REVIEW

E3 LEADERSHIP

E2 — EMPOWER YOUR PERFORMANCE

(E3.1) Discover Yourself

a) Know Your Personality
b) Know Your Powers
c) Know Your Purpose

DEVELOP YOURSELF

If I asked you, "What is your growth plan?" What would the response be? Would you be able to give me a quick and precise answer? If you hesitate or have to think hard about it, I have bad news for you…you probably don't have a growth plan.

The most successful companies and leaders know exactly what they are doing to help develop their people and themselves. They have thought through the process and implemented a system that creates a greenhouse effect of growth. They can tell you what their growth plan is very quickly and precisely because of the effort they have put into it.

You too should have a specific growth plan for yourself. Take some time to sit down and create a plan for how you are going to grow, or, if you already have a growth plan, sit down and reassess to see if there is anything you need to update within it.

I would also encourage you to theme out your growth plan around the specific areas you want to improve in. For example, if better communication is an area you want to grow in, rally around resources, speakers, conferences, leadership coaches, or anything that will help develop your communication skills. Do this for a few months as you keep the topic at the forefront of your focus. Always be investing into your leadership green-house and you'll always be improving your abilities.

Growth is essential for success. The more you develop yourself, the more opportunities will open up. When you raise your abilities, you'll raise your possibilities.

"When you raise your abilities, you'll raise your possibilities."

Here are three ways you can intentionally develop yourself: Get resources, get mentors, and get experiences.

GET RESOURCES

No one will ever grow to their maximum potential without reading. Reading great books, stories, biographies, articles, and blogs pertaining to your strengths is one of the fastest ways to grow on your journey. Take the wisdom and insights offered from others and apply it to your situation. To transform, the mind needs stimulation. One of the best ways to stimulate the mind is to read. It lets you soar on the wings of other people's great ideas and insights. If you could've spent a month with Steve Jobs for $24.95 would you have? If you could spend a week with Bill Gates for $14.95 would you? If you could spend six months with the top guru in your industry for just $19.95 would you? The truth is, you can. Get their resources and study their strategies and you'll gain their wisdom.

Leaders are readers. In fact, I have never met a highly success-ful person who is not an avid reader. Books are to the mind what nutrition is to the body. The more you dive into great books, the more growth you'll experience. American philosopher Mortimer Jerome Adler said, "In the case of good books, the point is not how many of them you can get through, but rather how many can get through to you." If you want inspiration, simply read. If you want information, study what you read. If you want transformation, act on what you read.

GET MENTORS

You can learn most everything you need in life by being around the right people. Finding mentors who will lift you to a higher level is vital for success.

People become like those they surround themselves with. What kind of people are you surrounding yourself with? Successful people are drawn to other successful people. They intentionally seek out those who are better and further along than they are themselves. One of the greatest traits of highly successful people is the drive to find and learn from people who are good at what they do. They go the extra mile to network with experts. We cannot reach our potential alone; we need others to help draw the best out of us.

Every leader needs a guide to help bring out the best in them. Luke had Yoda, Katniss had Haymitch, Frodo had Gandolph, Dorothy had Glenda, and the list goes on. Everyone needs a trusted coach to help them unleash the hero they were created to be. In almost every profession, high capacity individuals use a coach. Movie stars have acting coaches on set to help them in their roles. Singers have vocal coaches during recording sessions. Athletes have coaches during practices and on game day. And it's not just those starting out in their occupation. Seasoned professionals continue to use coaches for the longevity of their career. The fact is, having a coach helps bring out your very best.

GET EXPERIENCES

All experience is not created equal. Contrary to what you may have heard, experience is not the best teacher; educated experience is. There is a big difference between the two.

Experience doesn't teach you anything unless you take the time to learn from it. It is not enough to simply go through situations; you have to grow through situations. Just because someone goes through a difficult time does not necessarily mean they automatically learned from it. We all know people who have gone through a lot but have nothing to show from it. Educating yourself as to what you have acquired through your experiences will give you incredible insight into the future.

> "It's not what we've experienced that shapes us; it's what we've learned from our experiences that truly shape us."

It's not what we've experienced that shapes us; it's what we've learned from our experiences that truly shape us. Unless we take the time to reflect, we will be destined to repeat the past, or worse, forget about it. Every experience brings with it a seed of success. Don't allow yourself to waste experiences. Instead, take time to cultivate growth lessons from your experiences. Vernon Howard said, "Always walk through life as if you have something new to learn and you will."

REVIEW

E3 LEADERSHIP

E2 — EMPOWER YOUR PERFORMANCE

(E3.1) Discover Yourself

a) Know Your Personality
b) Know Your Powers
c) Know Your Purpose

(E3.2) Develop Yourself

a) Get Resources
b) Get Mentors
c) Get Experiences

DRIVE YOURSELF

The only limit you have is the belief you have one.

In 1906 football changed. The forward pass was legalized, but no one adopted the strategy. They clung to their traditional running and kicking. However, St. Louis University practiced the new play and implemented it. They outscored their opponents 402 to 11 that year and changed the game ever since. Like the University of St. Louis, we too, need to drive ourselves to embrace our future possibilities.

If you are going to empower your performance, you must drive yourself more so than anyone else. You can't wait for someone, or something to motivate you...that is your responsibility. You will never be who you want to be tomorrow if you don't start being who you want to be today.

Georges Clemenceau said, "A man who has to be convinced to act before he acts is not a man of action." Motivation happens when you do something motivational. If you wait for a feeling to hit you before you act, you may be waiting forever. We can't wait for the "feeling" in order to act; we must act our way into "feeling." When we step out and begin to do the things that will better us we will begin to get motivation.

If you are going to be a person of action that drives yourself you have to get disciplined, get determined, and get decisive.

GET DISCIPLINED

Albert Schweitzer said, "The tragedy of life is what dies inside a man while he lives." You don't want to be like the gravestone that read, "Died at 30…buried at 90."

Willpower is like a muscle; the more you use it, the bigger it gets. In fact, Charles Duhigg, author of *The Power of Habit* said, "As people strengthened their willpower muscles in one part of their lives—in the gym, or a money management program—that strength spilled over into what they ate or how hard they worked. Once willpower became stronger, it touched everything."

> "Willpower is like a muscle; the more you use it, the bigger it gets."

The more you use your willpower to change your outcome the more it will affect every area of your life for the good. But you will never develop strong willpower to overcome bad habits unless you start using some willpower. You don't have to start big. Start small and work your way up.

A friend of mine told me about a guy he was counseling that was very discouraged because he couldn't stop smoking cigarettes. Come to find out he went from 3 packs a day to just a few a cigarettes day, but he was still beating himself up for not being able to quit. 3 packs to 3 cigarettes a day is an amazing accomplishment that will eventually end up to no cigarettes at all.

If you wait to do something until you can do everything you won't do anything! Progressive discipline is the key to sustainability.

GET DETERMINED

If you are going to move towards the vision for your life, you'd better be ready for obstacles and challenges. There will always be roadblocks, and even detours, along your journey. You cannot get to the mountaintop of success without commitment and determination to the vision, no matter what the cost. Only climbing when you "feel like it," will never take you to new heights. You only get to the top through hard work and endurance. "Feeling like it" may get you started, but it won't keep you going.

When faced with obstacles and problems, many people are quick to give up. But to reach your destiny, you will always have to fight through setbacks and unforeseen challenges. Resistance is not a bad sign. It is actually a sign you are on the right path. Shake off the dust and get back up. Remember this: you cannot climb a smooth mountain. It is the rocky places that can be used to become better and stronger. If you only travel the familiar paths, you will never find the hidden treasures. Thomas Edison said, "When you have exhausted all possibilities, remember this–you haven't."

GET DECISIVE

To live life with intentionality, you must be decisive. Indecision to action kills opportunity. Analyzing every detail stalls forward progress. William Arthur Ward said, "The optimist lives on the peninsula of infinite possibilities; the pessimist is stranded on the island of perpetual indecision." Many people are stuck in the paralysis of analysis. They are drowning in a sea of distractions.

It is very difficult to be decisive when we are preoccupied with trying to figure out every reaction to our actions before we make a move. I am not saying we should act hastily, but most of us make excuses to talk ourselves out of acting at all. We get distracted by the details.

The word distraction means to be pulled apart. The word depicts a medieval type of torture method that would tear someone apart at the seams of their limbs by being tied to four horses going in opposite directions. This became known as Death by Dis-traction. We cannot allow ourselves to be distracted from the goals set before us. Everyone faces distractions in life, but the key is to identify them and to keep moving beyond them. Drive your performance in the straightest line possible to your target by eliminating the unnecessary.

Better to make a wrong decision decisively and recover than to make no decision at all.

REVIEW
E3 LEADERSHIP
E2 — EMPOWER YOUR PERFORMANCE

(E3.1) Discover Yourself
   a) Know Your Personality
   b) Know Your Powers
   c) Know Your Purpose

(E3.2) Develop Yourself
   a) Get Resources
   b) Get Mentors
   c) Get Experiences

(E3.3) Drive Yourself
   a) Get Disciplined
   b) Get Determined
   c) Get Decisive

Elevate Your Success

$\left(\text{E}\right)$

Elevate Your Success

Success is a very subjective term. In fact, if you were to line up ten different people, you would probably get ten different definitions. There is no one definition that success could hold to because it is what you make it to be.

So what is success?

If you haven't defined what success is for you how would you ever know if you've attained it?

The answer? You wouldn't know if you were successful, and you just might miss the fact that you are. The most successful people have clearly defined what success is for them. They are not ignorant of what it is they are trying to accomplish. It is a clear target that is meaningful to them. They know what they are doing in order to get to where they want to go. After all, we don't want to get to a destination only to find out it isn't what we wanted. Author Francis Chan said, "Our greatest fear should not be of failure but of succeeding at things in life that don't really matter."

The word success comes from the Latin word, "Succedere" meaning to go up, follow after, or come near. You have to know where you're going if you want to be successful. That may seem simple, but most people haven't clearly identified where they're going. You have to determine what targets you are aiming for so that you can go after them. Success must be defined by you and you alone. No one can hand you what success is; it is an internal definition that you have to formulate within yourself. It has to be your working definition.

And remember this, you will need to define success for the different domains of your life. Financial success is totally different than relational success. Relational success is very different from positional success. It's essential to have a definition of success for each category you desire to elevate. For every major category of your life, you need to be incredibly intentional about what you want to accomplish. Life is too short not to take it seriously.

Though you may have varying definitions of success for different areas of your life, the five things they should all have in common is: it must be simple, specific, strategic, scalable, and significant.

Here are some things to think about as you define what success is:

IT MUST BE SIMPLE

Success can't be complicated. It should be easily defined. Clare Boothe Luce, one of the first women to serve in the U.S. Congress, famously told President John F. Kennedy, "A great man is one sentence." One day when you're gone, your life will be summed up in a few words. The good news is you get to choose what those words will be about.

You have the opportunity to define what success is for you now. Don't overcomplicate the process. Clarity is accomplished by keeping things easily memorable. Keep it short and to the point. Albert Einstein said this about complexities, "If you can't explain it to a six-year-old, you don't understand it yourself." Your definition of success must be clearly recognized when you've achieved it.

IT MUST BE SPECIFIC

Success must be specifically measurable. It has to have a quantifiable outcome. To say that your definition for financial success is to be wealthier, doesn't cut it. It needs to be more like this example: To be debt free, with an annual income of $x, and giving x% to charity.

You must be able to know if you are living successfully. Saying you want to be wealthier, is like chasing infinity, how would you know if you caught it? The more specific you are, the better equipped you'll be to make it happen. It's incredible what activates inside of you when your mind locks on a particular target. Author Napoleon Hill said, "When your desires are strong enough, you will appear to possess superhuman powers to achieve."

IT MUST BE STRATEGIC

Success has to be an intentional endeavor. We can't treat success like little Johnny did. One day, little Johnny got his bow and arrows out to work on his target practice. He pulled arrows out of his quiver one by one and proceeded to shoot in every direction he felt like. He then would walk up to wherever the arrow had landed and draw a target right around it, making it a bull's eye every time. Several arrows and targets later, his sister said, "You don't do target practice that way. You draw the target, then shoot the arrow." Johnny responded: "I know that, but if you do it my way, you never miss!"

Unlike little Johnny, we can't just let our life go any direction it takes us and then draw a target around wherever we end up and call it a success. We need to be maximizing our potential by creating the success we desire. We have to be intentional about what our lives are about. Don't just throw random numbers, ideas, and metrics without knowing why you want to reach them. Many people throw arbitrary ideas out when defining success, but in order to make it count, be strategic about everything.

IT MUST BE SCALABLE

Yes, success must be attainable and practical, but it should also stretch you to scale higher than you've ever been. Success has to be something that challenges you to elevate. It must cause you to reach further than you've ever reached, and dream bigger than you've ever dreamt. In fact, if your dreams don't scare you, you're probably not dreaming big enough. Your definition should stretch you to greater heights. Artist Michelangelo said, "The greatest danger for most of us is not that our aim is too high and we miss it, but that it is too low and we reach it." Your definition of success should be just out of reach of what you currently can do, so it causes you to scale up to a higher level.

Never belittle your dreams because of an inner fear that tells you it's too much. Dare to believe in yourself.

IT MUST BE SIGNIFICANT

Success must embody a worthy cause. At the end of our life, we will have wanted to make a significant impact in the world. We will have wanted to know our life mattered somehow, someway. There was an old country song written years ago called *Live Like You Were Dying*. In it, county music star Tim McGraw encouraged us to live life to the fullest with no regrets. It received many accolades, including a Grammy Award for song of the year. Regardless if you liked the song or not, it had a powerful message.

We all need to awaken the desire inside of us to make every day count. We must know that our effort is successful in order to live life to the fullest. The only way for us to know this is to make our definition of success deserving of a significant impact. Make sure you leave a legacy because of the difference you desire to make. Only living for yourself is a very lonely life. Henry Ford said, "A business that makes nothing but money is a poor business."

Take some time to sit down and craft your definitions of success for each area of your life. Don't rush through it, but be methodical about it. The first step to being highly successful is to know what it is you are trying to do.

Conclusion

Thanks for journeying through E3 Leadership. I hope it has helped you somehow, someway, to go a new level in your leadership ability. I have found that when you invest in your leadership ability, you're directly investing in the future you desire to experience.

Great leaders are always advancing their leadership ability to the next level. They never stop challenging themselves to reach new heights. They know the secret to success is the capacity to lead well. In fact, true success is simply an overflow of great leadership. Yet, so many leaders and organizations feel frustratingly stuck. They are striving for success but aren't gaining any traction into growth. Their solution…work harder. But in doing so, they are just spinning their wheels in the mud.

This is where I come in. I help individuals and companies breakthrough their limiting factors and elevate their success. A Hay Group study of Fortune 500 companies found that 21%–40% utilize Executive Coaching; Coaching was used as standard leadership development for elite executives and talented up-and-comers. An internal report of the Personnel Management Association showed that when training is combined with coaching, individuals increase their productivity by an average of 86% compared to 22% with training alone.

I have been working with leaders for over eighteen years. I have been personally mentored by the #1 leadership expert in the world, Dr. John C. Maxwell, as a certified coach, speaker, and trainer on the John Maxwell Team. I have worked with fortune 5,000 companies, entrepreneurs, non-profits, and individuals who have leveled up their success through my coaching.

I would love the opportunity to help you and/or your team develop their leadership capacity. Please check out my website with great leadership tips updated weekly and get a free copy of my book 50 Powerful Quotes To Take You Somewhere Better.

If you would like to level up through coaching/training here is the process to get started:

CONTACT ME

Set up a time so we can connect and discover what the next level is for you, your team, and your organization. We will engage with your specific leadership challenges and needs, in order to move upward together. Email: John@johnbarrettleadership.com

CUSTOMIZE YOUR EXPERIENCE

My leadership coaching is designed to take you from exactly where you are to the next level. You will not find prepackaged and predetermined routines, but rather a leadership plan customized to fit your unique situations.

COACH YOUR LEADERSHIP

Once we have discovered your challenges and customized your plan, we will start to empower your leadership performance.

This is where the magic happens as we deliver leadership coaching that will get you to the next level.

CLIMB TO NEW LEVELS

When leaders go to a whole new level, their success goes to a whole new level. Investing in your leadership development will increase your impact, influence, ideas, and income. Being coached allows you to soar to new heights.

ABOUT THE AUTHOR

John is a sought after leadership coach, speaker, and trainer. He has been living and teaching leadership for over sixteen years. John has been personally mentored by world renown leadership expert, Dr. John C. Maxwell, and a host of other highly successful leaders. He has coached Fortune 5000 companies, entrepreneurs, non-profits, and individuals who desire to level up their success.

John has been interviewed on radio programs, podcasts, blogs, and many other platforms, reaching over 200,000 listeners. He is dedicated to guiding others to the next level on their leadership journey.

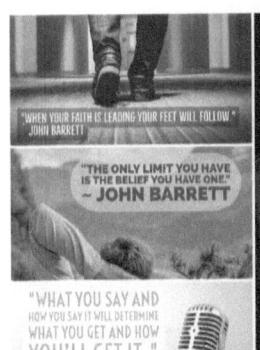

5 Ways To Get A Raise

"Truly Amazing!"
~ Jennifer Staggs (Account Executive)

"Book him today...for your next event!"
~ Chad Malone (Founder of Best Foot Forward Co.)

"John Barrett knows and understands leadership."
~ Ryan Goodwin (County Commissioner)

What People Are Saying About John's Talks...

- ✓ Dynamic Communication
- ✓ Insightful Content
- ✓ Memorable Experience
- ✓ Motivational Style
- ✓ Practical Tips
- ✓ Challenging Advice
- ✓ Heartfelt Passion
- ✓ Relevant Illustrations

"John Barrett has many talents to elevate your team to great success! If you want results he is sure to bring you that plus much more! I have known him now for a couple years and so glad that I do; he brings high energy and passion to every opportunity! Book him today...for your next event!"

~ Chad Malone
Founder of Best Foot Forward Co.

"John Barrett is truly an inspiration. His motivation and enthusiasm are contagious. He has presented at various events that I have attended over the years, and his message and presentation were fitting for all audiences. I can say without a doubt that you will be moved with his presentation."

~ Angela Kath
Relationship Manager

 WWW.JOHNBARRETTLEADERSHIP.COM

JohnBarrett
Leadership

NOTES

NOTES